HAL•LEONARD
INSTRUMENTAL
PLAY-ALONG

AUDIO
ACCESS
INCLUDED

PLAYBACK+
Speed • Pitch • Balance • Loop

CELLO

D0503925

Simple Songs

Audio arrangements by Peter Deneff

To access audio visit:
www.halleonard.com/mylibrary

Enter Code
3266-5633-4205-7570

ISBN 978-1-5400-0455-0

7777 W. BLUEMOUND RD. P.O. BOX 13819 MILWAUKEE, WI 53213

For all works contained herein:
Unauthorized copying, arranging, adapting, recording, Internet posting, public performance,
or other distribution of the printed or recorded music in this publication is an infringement of copyright.
Infringers are liable under the law.

Visit Hal Leonard Online at
www.halleonard.com

ALL OF ME

CELLO

Words and Music by JOHN STEPHENS
and TOBY GAD

Copyright © 2013 John Legend Publishing, EMI April Music Inc. and Gad Songs, LLC
All Rights for John Legend Publishing Administered by BMG Rights Management (US) LLC
All Rights for EMI April Music Inc. and Gad Songs, LLC Administered by Sony/ATV Music Publishing LLC, 424 Church Street, Suite 1200, Nashville, TN 37219
All Rights Reserved   Used by Permission

CAN YOU FEEL THE LOVE TONIGHT

from THE LION KING

CELLO

Music by ELTON JOHN
Lyrics by TIM RICE

© 1994 Wonderland Music Company, Inc.
All Rights Reserved. Used by Permission.

CAN'T HELP FALLING IN LOVE

from the Paramount Picture BLUE HAWAII

Cello

Words and Music by GEORGE DAVID WEISS,
HUGO PERETTI and LUIGI CREATORE

Copyright © 1961; Renewed 1989 Gladys Music (ASCAP)
All Rights in the U.S. Administered by Imagem Sounds and Songs Of Steve Peter
International Copyright Secured   All Rights Reserved

EVERMORE
from BEAUTY AND THE BEAST

Music by ALAN MENKEN
Lyrics by TIM RICE

CELLO

© 2017 Wonderland Music Company, Inc.
All Rights Reserved. Used by Permission.

HALLELUJAH

CELLO

Words and Music by
LEONARD COHEN

Copyright © 1985 Sony/ATV Music Publishing LLC
All Rights Administered by Sony/ATV Music Publishing LLC, 424 Church Street, Suite 1200, Nashville, TN 37219
International Copyright Secured   All Rights Reserved

HAPPY
from DESPICABLE ME 2

CELLO

Words and Music by
PHARRELL WILLIAMS

Copyright © 2013 EMI April Music Inc., More Water From Nazareth and Universal Pictures Global Music
All Rights on behalf of EMI April Music Inc. and More Water From Nazareth Administered by
Sony/ATV Music Publishing LLC, 424 Church Street, Suite 1200, Nashville, TN 37219
All Rights on behalf of Universal Pictures Global Music Controlled and Administered by Universal Music Works
International Copyright Secured   All Rights Reserved

HEY, SOUL SISTER

CELLO

Words and Music by PAT MONAHAN,
ESPEN LIND and AMUND BJORKLUND

Copyright © 2009 EMI April Music Inc., Blue Lamp Music and Stellar Songs Ltd.
All Rights Administered by Sony/ATV Music Publishing LLC, 424 Church Street, Suite 1200, Nashville, TN 37219
International Copyright Secured   All Rights Reserved

I GOTTA FEELING

CELLO

Words and Music by WILL ADAMS,
ALLAN PINEDA, JAIME GOMEZ,
STACY FERGUSON, DAVID GUETTA
and FREDERIC RIESTERER

Copyright © 2009 BMG Sapphire Songs, Will.I.Am Music Inc., Jeepney Music Publishing, Tab Magnetic Publishing,
EMI April Music Inc., Headphone Junkie Publishing, Square Rivoli Publishing and Rister Editions
All Rights for BMG Sapphire Songs, Will.I.Am Music Inc., Jeepney Music Publishing and Tab Magnetic Publishing Administered by BMG Rights Management (US) LLC
All Rights for EMI April Music Inc. and Headphone Junkie Publishing Administered by Sony/ATV Music Publishing LLC, 424 Church Street, Suite 1200, Nashville, TN 37219
All Rights for Square Rivoli Publishing and Rister Editions in the U.S. Administered by Shapiro, Bernstein & Co. Inc.
All Rights Reserved   Used by Permission

I'M YOURS

CELLO

Words and Music by
JASON MRAZ

Copyright © 2008 Goo Eyed Music (ASCAP)
International Copyright Secured   All Rights Reserved

LAVA
from LAVA

Words and Music by
JAMES FORD MURPHY

CELLO

© 2015 Walt Disney Music Company and Pixar Talking Pictures
All Rights Reserved. Used by Permission.

MY HEART WILL GO ON
(Love Theme From 'Titanic')
from the Paramount and Twentieth Century Fox Motion Picture TITANIC

CELLO

Music by JAMES HORNER
Lyric by WILL JENNINGS

Copyright © 1997 Sony/ATV Harmony, Sony/ATV Melody, T C F Music Publishing, Inc., Fox Film Music Corporation and Blue Sky Rider Songs
All Rights on behalf of Sony/ATV Harmony and Sony/ATV Melody Administered by Sony/ATV Music Publishing LLC, 424 Church Street, Suite 1200, Nashville, TN 37219
All Rights on behalf of Blue Sky Rider Songs Administered by Irving Music, Inc.
International Copyright Secured   All Rights Reserved

ROLLING IN THE DEEP

CELLO

Words and Music by ADELE ADKINS
and PAUL EPWORTH

Copyright © 2010, 2011 MELTED STONE PUBLISHING LTD. and EMI MUSIC PUBLISHING LTD.
All Rights for MELTED STONE PUBLISHING LTD. in the U.S. and Canada Controlled and Administered by
UNIVERSAL - SONGS OF POLYGRAM INTERNATIONAL, INC.
All Rights for EMI MUSIC PUBLISHING LTD. Administered by SONY/ATV MUSIC PUBLISHING LLC, 424 Church Street, Suite 1200, Nashville, TN 37219
All Rights Reserved   Used by Permission

VIVA LA VIDA

CELLO

Words and Music by GUY BERRYMAN,
JON BUCKLAND, WILL CHAMPION
and CHRIS MARTIN

Copyright © 2008 by Universal Music Publishing MGB Ltd.
All Rights in the United States and Canada Administered by Universal Music - MGB Songs
International Copyright Secured   All Rights Reserved

YOU RAISE ME UP

CELLO

Words and Music by BRENDAN GRAHAM
and ROLF LOVLAND

Copyright © 2002 by Peermusic (UK) Ltd. and Universal Music Publishing, A Division of Universal Music AS
All Rights for Peermusic (UK) Ltd. in the United States Controlled and Administered by Peermusic III, Ltd.
All Rights for Universal Music Publishing, A Division of Universal Music AS in the United States and Canada
Controlled and Administered by Universal - PolyGram International Publishing, Inc. (Publishing) and Alfred Music (Print)
International Copyright Secured   All Rights Reserved

HAL•LEONARD INSTRUMENTAL PLAY-ALONG

Your favorite songs are arranged just for solo instrumentalists with this outstanding series. Each book includes a great full-accompaniment play-along audio so you can sound just like a pro! Check out www.halleonard.com to see all the titles available.

The Beatles

All You Need Is Love • Blackbird • Day Tripper • Eleanor Rigby • Get Back • Here, There and Everywhere • Hey Jude • I Will • Let It Be • Lucy in the Sky with Diamonds • Ob-La-Di, Ob-La-Da • Penny Lane • Something • Ticket to Ride • Yesterday.

_____	00225330	Flute	$14.99
_____	00225331	Clarinet	$14.99
_____	00225332	Alto Sax	$14.99
_____	00225333	Tenor Sax	$14.99
_____	00225334	Trumpet	$14.99
_____	00225335	Horn	$14.99
_____	00225336	Trombone	$14.99
_____	00225337	Violin	$14.99
_____	00225338	Viola	$14.99
_____	00225339	Cello	$14.99

Chart Hits

All About That Bass • All of Me • Happy • Radioactive • Roar • Say Something • Shake It Off • A Sky Full of Stars • Someone like You • Stay with Me • Thinking Out Loud • Uptown Funk.

_____	00146207	Flute	$12.99
_____	00146208	Clarinet	$12.99
_____	00146209	Alto Sax	$12.99
_____	00146210	Tenor Sax	$12.99
_____	00146211	Trumpet	$12.99
_____	00146212	Horn	$12.99
_____	00146213	Trombone	$12.99
_____	00146214	Violin	$12.99
_____	00146215	Viola	$12.99
_____	00146216	Cello	$12.99

Coldplay

Clocks • Every Teardrop Is a Waterfall • Fix You • In My Place • Lost! • Paradise • The Scientist • Speed of Sound • Trouble • Violet Hill • Viva La Vida • Yellow.

_____	00103337	Flute	$12.99
_____	00103338	Clarinet	$12.99
_____	00103339	Alto Sax	$12.99
_____	00103340	Tenor Sax	$12.99
_____	00103341	Trumpet	$12.99
_____	00103342	Horn	$12.99
_____	00103343	Trombone	$12.99
_____	00103344	Violin	$12.99
_____	00103345	Viola	$12.99
_____	00103346	Cello	$12.99

Disney Greats

Arabian Nights • Hawaiian Roller Coaster Ride • It's a Small World • Look Through My Eyes • Yo Ho (A Pirate's Life for Me) • and more.

_____	00841934	Flute	$12.99
_____	00841935	Clarinet	$12.99
_____	00841936	Alto Sax	$12.99
_____	00841937	Tenor Sax	$12.95
_____	00841938	Trumpet	$12.99
_____	00841939	Horn	$12.99
_____	00841940	Trombone	$12.95
_____	00841941	Violin	$12.99
_____	00841942	Viola	$12.99
_____	00841943	Cello	$12.99
_____	00842078	Oboe	$12.99

Great Themes

Bella's Lullaby • Chariots of Fire • Get Smart • Hawaii Five-O Theme • I Love Lucy • The Odd Couple • Spanish Flea • and more.

_____	00842468	Flute	$12.99
_____	00842469	Clarinet	$12.99
_____	00842470	Alto Sax	$12.99
_____	00842471	Tenor Sax	$12.99
_____	00842472	Trumpet	$12.99
_____	00842473	Horn	$12.99
_____	00842474	Trombone	$12.99
_____	00842475	Violin	$12.99
_____	00842476	Viola	$12.99
_____	00842477	Cello	$12.99

Popular Hits

Breakeven • Fireflies • Halo • Hey, Soul Sister • I Gotta Feeling • I'm Yours • Need You Now • Poker Face • Viva La Vida • You Belong with Me • and more.

_____	00842511	Flute	$12.99
_____	00842512	Clarinet	$12.99
_____	00842513	Alto Sax	$12.99
_____	00842514	Tenor Sax	$12.99
_____	00842515	Trumpet	$12.99
_____	00842516	Horn	$12.99
_____	00842517	Trombone	$12.99
_____	00842518	Violin	$12.99
_____	00842519	Viola	$12.99
_____	00842520	Cello	$12.99

Songs from Frozen, Tangled and Enchanted

Do You Want to Build a Snowman? • For the First Time in Forever • Happy Working Song • I See the Light • In Summer • Let It Go • Mother Knows Best • That's How You Know • True Love's First Kiss • When Will My Life Begin • and more.

_____	00126921	Flute	$14.99
_____	00126922	Clarinet	$14.99
_____	00126923	Alto Sax	$14.99
_____	00126924	Tenor Sax	$14.99
_____	00126925	Trumpet	$14.99
_____	00126926	Horn	$14.99
_____	00126927	Trombone	$14.99
_____	00126928	Violin	$14.99
_____	00126929	Viola	$14.99
_____	00126930	Cello	$14.99

Top Hits

Adventure of a Lifetime • Budapest • Die a Happy Man • Ex's & Oh's • Fight Song • Hello • Let It Go • Love Yourself • One Call Away • Pillowtalk • Stitches • Writing's on the Wall.

_____	00171073	Flute	$12.99
_____	00171074	Clarinet	$12.99
_____	00171075	Alto Sax	$12.99
_____	00171106	Tenor Sax	$12.99
_____	00171107	Trumpet	$12.99
_____	00171108	Horn	$12.99
_____	00171109	Trombone	$12.99
_____	00171110	Violin	$12.99
_____	00171111	Viola	$12.99
_____	00171112	Cello	$12.99

Wicked

As Long As You're Mine • Dancing Through Life • Defying Gravity • For Good • I'm Not That Girl • Popular • The Wizard and I • and more.

_____	00842236	Flute	$12.99
_____	00842237	Clarinet	$12.99
_____	00842238	Alto Saxophone	$11.95
_____	00842239	Tenor Saxophone	$11.95
_____	00842240	Trumpet	$11.99
_____	00842241	Horn	$11.95
_____	00842242	Trombone	$12.99
_____	00842243	Violin	$11.99
_____	00842244	Viola	$12.99
_____	00842245	Cello	$12.99

Prices, contents, and availability subject to change without notice.
Disney characters and artwork © Disney Enterprises, Inc.